KU-051-286

First published in Great Britain in 1980 by Octopus Books Ltd

This edition published in 1984 by Treasure Press
59 Grosvenor Street
London W1

© 1980 Octopus Books Ltd

ISBN 0 907812 83 X

Printed in Hong Kong

Educational and Series advisor Felicia Law

MY FIRST COUNTING BOOK

by

Felicia Law and Suzanne Chandler

illustrated by
John Farman

TREASURE PRESS

Contents

Numbers 0 to 10

The Great Mouse Balancing Act

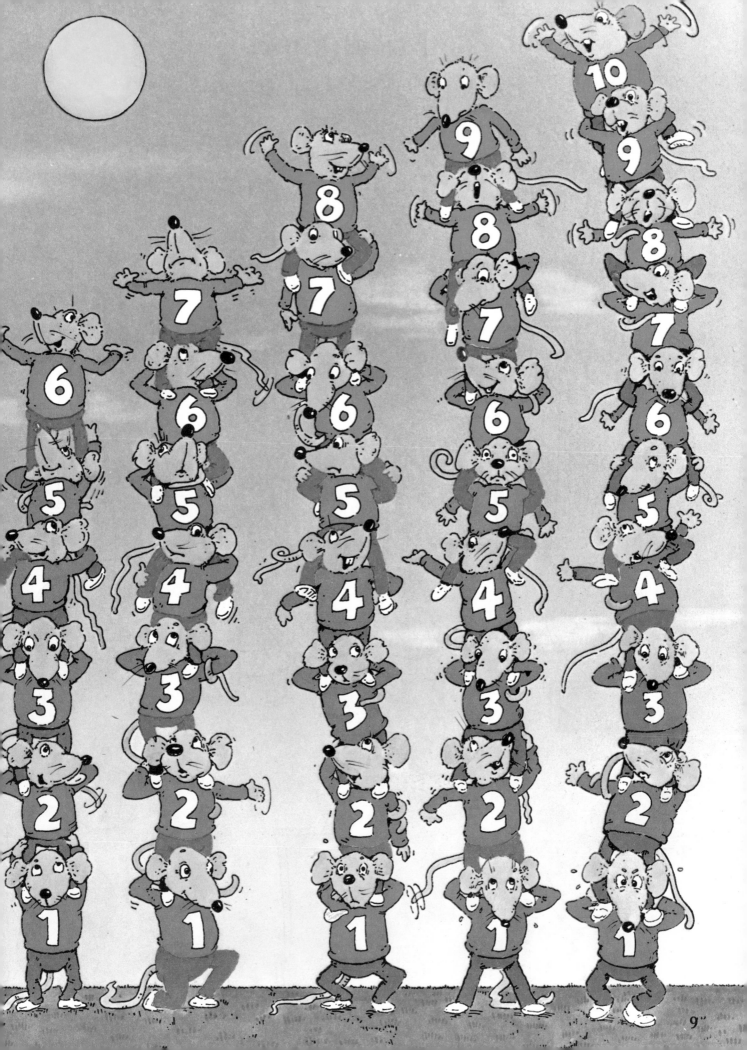

Matching

Match the numbers to the pictures

How Many?

How many mice are wearing spectacles?
How many red flowers can you see?
How many mice are wearing hats?
How many mice are wearing bow ties?

Counting Rhyme

A rhyme for you to learn and make up actions to.

ONE mouse in the bookcase
TWO mice on the hearth
THREE mice on the mantelpiece
FOUR mice take a bath
FIVE mice raid the larder
Eat the cottage cheese
SIX mice at the cellar door
Trying all the keys
SEVEN mice in a saucepan
EIGHT mice in a pie
NINE mice gulp a pancake
In the twinkling of an eye
TEN mice take siesta
Stomachs gorged and fat –
Scuttle down the mousehole
Or else you'll feed the cat!

Drawing Lines

Draw a line to enclose all the mice who are wearing boots and another to enclose those wearing knitted bobble hats. How many mice are wearing boots and bobble hats?

Missing Mice

These line-ups seem to be missing one or two mice. Put the correct mice back in the empty spaces

They are taking a short rest at the bottom of the page.

Mice Price – The best supermarket in town

This GRAPH shows the piles of bargains on the
supermarket shelves.
Can you see what is for sale?

Which piles are highest?
Where are stocks running low?

15

Smash 10
(You should be able to do this without a sledge hammer.)

$$1 + 9 = 10$$
$$2 + 8 = 10$$
$$3 + ? = 10$$

How many other ways can you smash up 10?

Balance the See-saw

How can the young mice get the see-saws to balance?
Add more mice to each plank where they are needed.

The Ten Gang

Big T. calls a meeting of the Ten Gang. "You're lucky to be here," he tells them all. "I'm pretty choosy."

"And," says Big T. firmly, "there is no room for expansion. Who ever heard of 'ten plus one'?"

"Actually," says eleven, "I have a smarter name than that."

"I suppose you have a smart name too," says Big T., "but that won't get you in either."

"At risk of repeating myself," says Big T., "this is the Ten Gang. Now you guys are welcome to hang around outside…

4

… and do a spot of careful figuring…

5

… but no matter how many of you keep on coming…"

But Big T. suddenly stopped talking when the ten mice he wouldn't let in walked off in a group. They were laughing and talking and calling themselves The Next Ten Gang!

The Abercrumbie Mouse Voice Choir

One sunny day, the Choir boarded the coach for the Micesteddford.

"That's the lot," said Dai, "nine tenors, one bass…

"It's only civil to give a hitch-hiker a lift," said Dai, " and we never let fans down

And he was right! It took everyone to move the coach…

...and Willie the Wheel.
Now how many is that?"

"Looks as if we've got another passenger,"
said Dai. "Now I'd better count again."

"You'd better count how many we've got on board," warned Willie the Wheel

"Because that's just the number we're going to need to push."

...and everyone to win the trophy.
And Dai is still counting...!

Patter and Pounce

This is the mousey way of playing Snakes and Ladders.
You will need a dice and one counter for each player.
Follow the numbers from 1 to 50 to find the winner.

The Great Mouse Toppling Act

Those strong little mice have been balancing on each other's shoulders ever since page 8. No wonder they are beginning to topple off. Starting with the base-man, COUNT BACKWARDS to find out how many mice are missing.

Little Red Riding Puss

Little Red Riding Puss set off through the woods to visit her dear old granny.
She had carefully packed ten cookies in her basket.

But unknown to her a pair of sharp teeth had already been at work.

One by one the cookies dropped out . COUNT DOWN from 10 as they drop.

Dear old granny was not at all pleased when she saw the empty basket.
She wrinkled her nose and chased Red Riding Puss all the way home.

27

Groups

1 mouse rides 2 wheels and juggles 3 balls
2 mice ride 4 wheels and juggle 6 balls
3 mice

Can you finish the last line?

28

The 3 Group

The busy window cleaner
has a long way
to go yet!

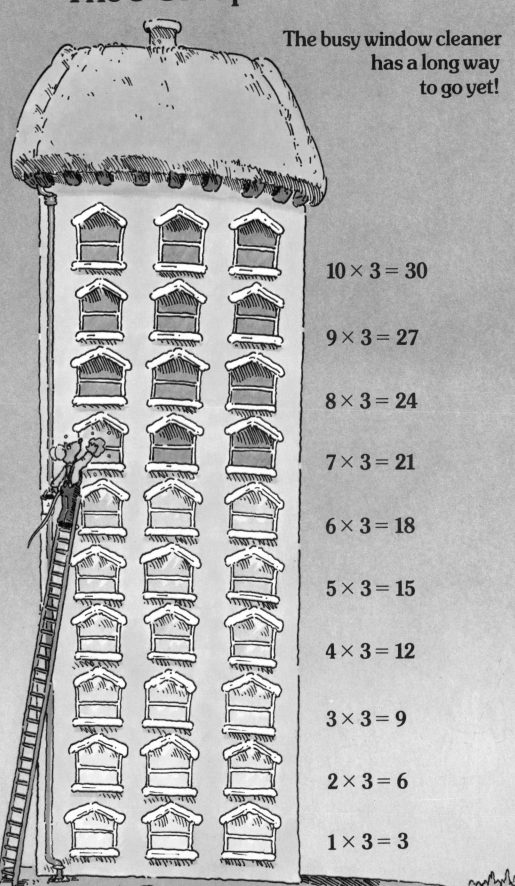

$10 \times 3 = 30$

$9 \times 3 = 27$

$8 \times 3 = 24$

$7 \times 3 = 21$

$6 \times 3 = 18$

$5 \times 3 = 15$

$4 \times 3 = 12$

$3 \times 3 = 9$

$2 \times 3 = 6$

$1 \times 3 = 3$

Picking the 4 Team

Use the answers in the multiplication table opposite to decide which players will get chosen for the 4 team.

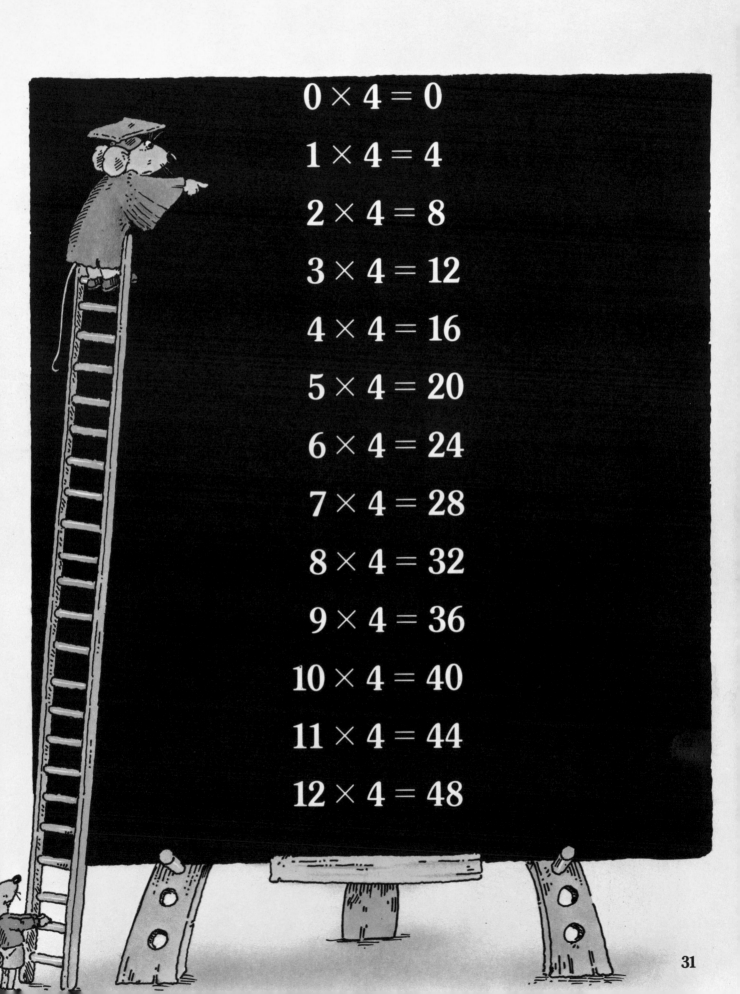

$0 \times 4 = 0$

$1 \times 4 = 4$

$2 \times 4 = 8$

$3 \times 4 = 12$

$4 \times 4 = 16$

$5 \times 4 = 20$

$6 \times 4 = 24$

$7 \times 4 = 28$

$8 \times 4 = 32$

$9 \times 4 = 36$

$10 \times 4 = 40$

$11 \times 4 = 44$

$12 \times 4 = 48$

Harvest Song

Farmer Brown is big and strong
He plants one furrow ten tails long
The sun and rain help every day
To grow five bales of golden hay.

Hey-down, how-down
Reap and sow-down
Who brings least
To the harvest feast?

Farmer Patch is old and wise
He plants his corn in
    two straight lines
The sun and rain help every day
To grow ten bales of golden hay.

Hey-down, how-down
Reap and sow-down
Who brings least
To the harvest feast?

Farmer Whiskers plans his yield
He plants three furrows in his field
The sun and rain help every day
To grow fifteen bales of golden hay.

Hey-down, how-down
Reap and sow-down
Who brings least
To the harvest feast?

The Pattern of 3

Colour in and number the 3 pattern.
You should notice something special about these numbers.

1	2		4	5		7	8		10
11		13	14		16	17		19	20
	22	23		25	26		28	29	
31	32		34	35		37	38		40
41		43	44		46	47		49	50
	52	53		55	56		58	59	
61	62		64	65		67	68		70
71		73	74		76	77		79	80
	82	83		85	86		88	89	
91	92		94	95		97	98		100

Dividing Means the Same as Sharing

When the cheese is shared out everyone must get an equal-sized chunk.

Anything left over is called the remainder.
Use this sign to show you are sharing out.

Even Numbers Make Pairs

The mice are whooping it up at the Summer Ball.
Numbers that divide by 2 make pairs.
Numbers that do not divide by 2 leave a spare dancer.

Even and Odd

Welcome to the match between
Mousechester United and Nibbling Wanderers.

Mousechester United are playing in the even numbers.
Nibbling Wanderers are playing in the odd numbers.

When the half time whistle blows the teams must leave
the field by the correct gate. Can you sort them out?

Who Went That A-way?

The mice of the Pawpaw tribe wear three feathers in their hair. Just how many of those wily natives have escaped the sheriff?

Sharing

This simple dividing sum is causing a great deal of argument. Can you help solve the problem?
Are there any nuts left over?

Buying Dinner

What a deliciously tempting meal you can get at the Stilton Hotel. Can you work out what Mr Mouse is going to pay for his selection? Why not join him?

Choose your food and work out how much the bill will come to.

The Stilton Hotel

Tomato soup	5
Ham	7
Beans	4
Egg	6
Chips	10
Cheese	9

Magic Squares

Add across the rows, down the rows, and diagonally, to get a surprising result.

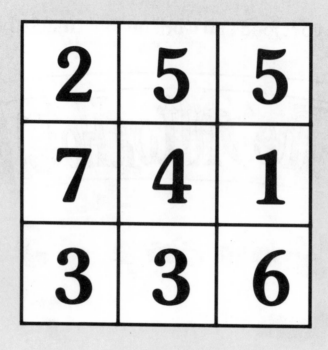

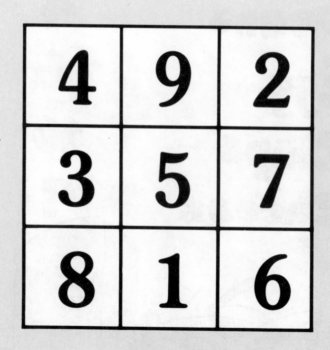

Doing Some Sums

Practise some of the number work you have learnt in this book by using a spinner top.

1 Cut a card hexagon as shown and mark the sections.

2 Stub a short pencil through the centre. Make sure it has a sharp point.

3 Place a saucer of dried peas (or equivalent) in the centre of the table.

COUNTING ON – Each child spins the top taking peas to match the number on which the top falls. The first child to have 20 peas is the winner.

COUNTING DOWN – Each player tries to get rid of 20 peas by the reverse method.

Use the spinner top to practise all the four rules of number.

Notes for Parents

Many innovations have affected the teaching of mathematics over the last ten years, but at this very early level the emphasis has shifted towards even greater practical and verbal experience. Consequently much early number work is based upon the child's experiences in the home. Games, songs, rhymes, sorting, matching and colouring activities have become an important part of the process of familiarizing young children with number concepts.

In this book we are not advocating that parents take over the role of teacher. There have been important changes in the methods of recording mathematics, not least in the vocabulary now employed, and it would be foolish to risk any confusion. MOUSE COUNT offers the parent rich scope for story telling and game playing on number themes. Although single examples are shown, many of the techniques can be adapted to demonstrate a quite different concept. Equally, parents should not be dismayed if the child dismisses the text or adapts the pictures to some more colourful explanation of his own. The charming illustrations in this book often tell their own story.

Although the book is intended as a shared verbal activity for parent and child, many children will wish to take up crayons and use it as a workbook. Parents may prefer to supply a pencil and pad of paper. In any case, the child should always be encouraged to copy or trace symbols and numbers for himself, if he shows any interest in so doing.

The following notes offer further ideas for linked activities.

NUMBER RECOGNITION pages 7 to 9
Use these domino shapes when illustrating number (p7) keeping carefully to the same patterns.
Fill a basin with an assortment of objects. Let the child sort them into matching groups then count each group.
Talk about the graph on p8 and 9. Discuss 'more than' and 'less than.'

COUNTING pages 11 to 15
Find family groups, as on page 11, in old wedding photographs, seaside groups, etc. Sort and count. Invent body actions to accompany the rhyme (p12), peeping, warming hands by fire, scrubbing back in bath, and so on.
When sorting and matching, discuss groups or similar objects or sets. Find objects common to more than one set.
Use the basin of small objects to find sets.
Discuss the place value of the missing numbers (p14). Make sure the child understands the correct sequence of numbers. Use the graph on page 15 to reinforce counting, 'less than,' 'greater than.'

ADDITION pages 16 to 23
Smash up other numbers besides 10 to emphasize addition. Discuss the see-saw balance as addition by counting on, and later as subtraction. (How many mice stepped off the plank?)
Discuss the story on pages 18 and 19 to illustrate the value of 10 units as 1 ten.
Discuss the value of two lots of ten making twenty.

SUBTRACTION pages 24 to 27
Introduce as counting down.
Play games involving 'loss,' hiding or 'how much more?'

MULTIPLICATION pages 28 to 34
Emphasize patterns and groups of numbers and *not* the rhythm of multiplication tables. Stimulate curiosity in the shape of any multiplication table within the 100 square (p34). Discuss odd and even numbers and pairs.
Discuss the fate of the 'remainder.'

DIVISION pages 35 to 39
Discuss as sharing out.
Play SNAP, HAPPY FAMILIES, grouping cards into pairs or fours.
Encourage children to deal cards among players.
Encourage children to share sweets, etc.

ACTIVITIES pages 40 to 42
More and more children handle small value coins at an early age. The metric base to our money system obviously helps young children to understand the value of 10. It is easier to 'smash' 10 using actual coins than to 'smash' ten units using written symbols, therefore any kind of shopping experience is useful.

The spinning top can be converted to provide experience in all four rules. Divisions can be marked $+2$, $+5$, $+1$ etc. or -2, -5, -1 etc. or a combination may be used.